BROKEN BUT YET FIXED

"THE BATTLE WITHIN"

SHANIKA SHUMPERT

For permission requests, write to the publisher, addressed "Attention: Permissions Coordinator," at the address below.

Broken But Yet Fixed Ministry
PO Box 618
New Albany, Mississippi 38652

Bokenbutyetfixedministry@gmail.com

Editor: Shanika Shumpert, [ShanikaShumpert@gmail.com]
Interior designer: Shanika Shumpert,
Shumpert, Shumpert. M.

ISBN: 978-0-578-90896-0

BROKEN BUT YET FIXED

"THE BATTLE WITHIN"

SHANIKA SHUMPERT

THE BATTLE WITHIN

When I was a child, I spoke as a child, I understood as a child, I thought as a child; but when I became a man, I put away childish things (1 Corinthians 13:11 NKJV).

A WORD FROM GOD

Everyone who is called by My name, whom I have created for My glory; I have formed him, yes, I have made him. These people I have formed for Myself; They shall declare My praise (Isaiah 43:7,21 NKJV).

DEDICATION & ACKNOWLEDGMENTS

I want to first start by thanking God Almighty, who is the head of my life. I will forever be grateful, and I will always give you praise.

I want to thank my sister from another mother, Tina Brooks, my number one support for always encouraging and uplifting me.

I also want to thank my amazing children, Ariel, Brian, and Braxton and my nephews and nieces that I love dearly.

Much thanks to my spiritual sister Judy Fry. Words can't explain how grateful I am for having you as a true friend. May God continue to bless you, coming in and going out always and forever. Amen

Now, Mario Wallace, I hope you didn't think I would leave you out of this. Thank God for your help. You helped me when no one else would, and I am thankful for that.

Contents

Recovering from the battle within------------------------13

Chapter I: Healing and Deliverance------------------------15

Healing Within--17

Healing Scriptures--19

Healing Prayer--21

Chapter II: The Important of Growth----------------------22

Crayon--23

Chapter III: The Important of Prayer----------------------25

The Lord Prayer--27

Going to God in prayer--28

Chapter IV: Examine Yourselves--------------------------29

You have not failed the test----------------------------------30

Learning to grow spiritually----------------------------------31

Count it all Joy--32

Encouraging Quotes--33

Examine Yourself First--34

Chapter V: Forgiveness------------------------------------36

Forgiveness Scripture--38

Forgiveness Prayer---39

Chapter VI: Separation------------------------------------40

Unity of the Faith---44

Isolation--45

Chapter VII: Deliverance through Christ Jesus----------46

David Forgiveness Prayer to the Lord--------------------------48

David ask God to cleanse him from his sin---------------------50

David give God praise for his forgiveness----------------------52

Deliverance Scripture--54

What is a Deliverance prayer? ----------------------------------56

Deliverance Prayer--58

Chapter VIII: Preparation---------------------------------------60

The whole armor of God--62

Revelation---63

RECOVERING FROM THE BATTLE WITHIN

We all, in some sense, have battled with turmoil in our life. The most important part "is knowing who we are and who we serve." We tend to run into problems often. As the issues arise, we try to fix them or cover them up. Instead of giving them to God, we often think we know what is better for us than God does. We tend to put God on the back burner and try to fix it ourselves.

I've learned that all battles are not our battles to fight (2 Chronicles 20:15-17 NKJV). If only we knew the concept, fight your battles on your knees in secret, early in life (Ephesians 6:12 NKJV).

Every day is a journey, new problems, new blessings, new decision-making, etc. Dealing with life's struggle is a battle within ourselves that we face or will face at some point in our lives. The hardest part is trying to get through it and finding the proper help.

The worse part is accepting that some people will not get the help they need, and some will refuse the help. Life is full of surprises. When dealing with a sickness or facing death, it hits hard in that person's life, but how a person deals with it depends on their mindset and relationship with God.

I am praying this book will help guide you through your struggle to find yourself and, most of all, teach you how to build a relationship with God. My purpose for writing this book is to encourage someone who may be on the journey of healing and deliverance.

CHAPTER 1

HEALING AND DELIVERANCE

Healing and deliverance is the most important step into becoming a better person. While you are on the road to recovery, you cannot do anything without God (John 15:5 NKJV). Let's just gone and put that on the front line. I repeat, **YOU CAN NOT DO NOTHING WITHOUT GOD.** With God, all things are possible. Healing comes from within.

Deliverance comes when you recognize your wrongdoing, confess with your mouth, and ask for forgiveness (Romans 10:9 NKJV).

Do not be ashamed of your struggles; walk in them with pride. Any battle that you face is designed to make you stronger where you are weak and to draw you closer to God (1 Peter 4:16 NKJV); If you run across a person without struggles in their life, run as fast as you can because something is not right about them.

Your first step in healing and deliverance is to build a relationship with God. First, you must go to God in prayer and ask Him to forgive you for all your wrongdoing that you have done knowingly and unknowingly. Next, you forgive people that have wrong you. Then, accept all your wrongdoing by owning up to it (col 3:13 NKJV).

Everyone knows a genuinely spiritual person. Reach out to them and make them your mentor. Begin to search for a church home if you don't already have one. Remove yourself from harmful environments.

Don't be too quick to share your experience with others because some people will not understand you, which could cause you to have doubt. So, it's best to go to your closet in secret with God and continue praying and asking God to strengthen where you are weak.

And always remember that you have to encourage yourself during a raging storm in your life (1 Samuel 30:6 NKJV).

HEALING WITHIN

Healing is like a deep penetrating wound that sometimes is a long healing process, and sometimes it take years to recover. Some wounds never heal. Why? Because sometimes, we don't know how to heal on our own. When taking care of an injury, you must follow doctor's orders on treating it daily, whether it's cleaning it, dressing it, or keeping pressure off it, or applying pressure to it.

Some wounds get infected, meaning something went wrong in the healing process. For example, when we are going through the healing process, we begin to grow bitter, angry, become distant, and some even isolate themselves from the world causing them to stop living their lives and start living in guilt resulting a mental break down (2 Corinthians 1:3-11 NKJV).

If you ever had a wound, you know exactly how the pain feels; Sometimes, it is unbearable to the point that you wish death upon yourself (Isaiah 41:10 NKJV). The healing process is the same. You will get to a point where it seems like all hope is gone and feel as if there is no point in living anymore. You might begin to think of ways to take your life. This phrase is where you have let your emotions take over (Psalm 147:3-5).

It reminds me of the saying, "don't let the devil ride because then he will want to drive." We all have felt pain in our life to the point we thought we wouldn't heal from it (Psalm 34:18 NKJV). We have all faced hard times whether it's losing a loved one, getting a divorce, going through a bad break-up, losing a job, financial debt, living from paycheck to paycheck, children in and out of trouble, family and friends not available when you needed them most. All of the aforementioned can be detrimental to the average person, but one must have faith and trust in God.

God said he wouldn't put any more on us than we can bear in time of trouble (1 Corinthians 10:13 NKJV).

HEALING SCRIPTURES

Remember, God wants his children well! On your walk with God, always remember to keep his word close to your heart. God's word will help you through life's struggles. We must familiarize ourselves with the word of God and focus on building a closer relationship with him because it will play an essential role in our life. It's like working on an assembly line. You can't leave any parts out, each piece plays a significant role in assembly of the finished product, and it must be done right by the assembler. We should be like this when it comes to our walk with God; our walk with God plays an essential part in our lives.

I pulled a few scriptures to help you get an idea of God divine healing; you will find them below:

Heal me, O'Lord, and I shall be healed; save me, and I shall be saved, for you are my praise (Jeremiah 17:14 NKJV).

Fear not, for I am with you; be not dismayed, for I am your God; I will strengthen you, help you, and uphold you with my righteous right hand (Isaiah 41:10 NKJV).

Behold, I will bring it to health and healing, and I will heal them and reveal to them the abundance of prosperity and security (Jeremiah 33:6 NKJV).

Bless the Lord, O my soul, and forget not all his benefits, who forgives all your iniquity, who heals all your diseases, who redeems your life from the pit, who crowns you with steadfast love and mercy (Psalm 103:2-4 NKJV).

HEALING PRAYER

Father, the God of Abraham, Isaac, and Jacob, your word declares if we would humble ourselves and pray and seek your face, then we will hear from heaven. Father, I come to you right now as one of your broken children. I come to you asking for your divine healing in my life. I know that I have not done right by you. I ask for your forgiveness. Lord, I ask that you come into my life and clean me up. Lord, show me how to get back on the right pathway. I have tried everything, and nothing seems to help. I have learned that I was doing everything the wrong way, and it was not pleasing to you. I was trying to live a life without you. I know that without you, I am nothing, Lord. I ask you to come into my life, clean me up, renew my mind, renew my spirit, renew my strength. Lord, I want to live a life pleasing to you and not man. Create in me a clean heart. Bless me with your wisdom, knowledge, and understanding. Lord, send your angels to surround me and keep me safe and protected, keep me away from all hurt, harm, and danger while I'm on this journey of chasing after you. In your Son Jesus name. Amen.

CHAPTER II

THE IMPORTANCE OF GROWTH

Growth is vital part of the healing stage. The separation will begin to occur in this process. You start to look over your past and compare it to your current situation while figuring out where you go from here.

You begin to question yourself. You will feel as if you are trapped in the circle of confusion. It's very similar to driving a remote- control car with the attached wiring. You can only go so far before you start getting resistance, and you begin to back up a little and steer the wheel in another direction (running away or giving up).

We must learn how to identify the problem and fix it. If you know you can't do it and need help. Don't be afraid to ask someone that you trust for guidance (Job 8:7 NKJV) (2 Peter 3:18 NKJV) (1 Timothy 4:15NKJV) (Hebrew 5:12-14 NKJV).

CRAYON

I want you to imagine that you are holding a box of crayons in your hand. Now, open it up. You will see all sorts of colors in the box. We are just like this box of crayons; we come in all different colors, we all endure and face the same problems, pain, issues, and losses throughout life.

I remember as a child when my crayon would break while coloring, I would find tape and tape it back together. Reusing it, not realizing as I began to color it will loosen back up and eventually fall apart again.

As adults, we do the same when problems come in our lives; we try to do a quick fix, not realizing it only works for a moment.

When the problem that was temporarily fixed begins to fall apart again, you feel as if your life is falling apart. The emotional stress can send one on an emotional roller coaster or into a depressing state of mind. And no matter what color you are, we all got to go through something. Fact is we are going to suffer a little on this earth (1 Peter 5:10 NJKV) (John 16:33 NKJV) (1Cor 10:13 NKJV) (Romans 8:18 NJKV).

Because some of us have so much pride (Prov 16:18 NKJV) (Gal 6:3 NKJV), we cover up our hurt and pain. Some walk around like they're built like a Tonka truck, can sustain any damage and still be ok. Some people try to hold steadfast, not knowing this is destroying them on the inside slowly, causing them to feel some way toward others.

It is so important to know who God is and how to pray. If you don't get anything out of reading this book, remember this: reading God's word and getting to know God plays a significant role in our life. We must learn how to apply God's word in our everyday living (Mark 12:30 NKJV) (Mat 22:37 NKJV) (John 15:5,16 NKJV).

CHAPTER III

THE IMPORTANCE OF PRAYER

Be anxious for nothing, but in everything by prayer and supplication with thanksgiving, let your requests be made known to God (Philippians 4:6 NKJV). Not knowing how to pray is the number one concern in people's lives today. Many people don't know how to pray. God has given us a model prayer to pray in (Matthew 6: 9-13 NKJV) and (Luke 11: 2-4). He has given us an ideal outline of how to pray for new beginners.

As you grow closer to God, you begin to spend more time reading and praying. You will notice a change in yourself and how people start to treat you differently, and that's ok! Stay focus! Keep your mind clear (Philippians 2:5 NKJV); Keep your circle small. Remember, when you choose God and begin to follow him, things will start to shift in your life. Don't be afraid (Psalm 37:7-8 NKJV).

When God begins to move people and things(habits) out of your life, don't be surprised. When this happens, you continue to pray by asking God to continue to remove anything in your life that's not of him.

No matter what you are going through, know that God has your back. (Ephesians 6:11-17 NKJV) I'm so glad that God is not like man. Instead of kicking you while you down, God will pick you right back up and put you back on the right pathway.

(Ephesians 6:18 NKJV) tell us to always pray with all prayer and supplication in the spirit (**take everything to God in prayer**) and watching thereunto with all perseverance and supplication for all saints.

On our walk with Christ Jesus, the number one thing you will learn is how to wait on the Lord patiently.

THE LORD PRAYER

Our Father, which art in heaven,

Hallowed by the name.

Thy kingdom come.

Thy will be done in earth,

As it is in heaven.

Give us this day our daily bread,

And forgive of our debts,

As we forgive our debtors.

And lead us not into temptation,

But deliver us from evil:

For thy is the kingdom,

And power and glory

Forever.

Amen

(Matthew 6:9 -13 NKJV)

GOING TO GOD IN PRAYER

When going to God in prayer, understand you will have a part that you must do in this process. Because you have turned it over to God, understand you will need to work on yourself. You will first start by doing a self-evaluation of yourself. If you want God to move mountains for you, you must be willing to work on your relationship with Him. You can start by reading his word and praying daily (1 Corinthians 15:52-54 NKJV).

Learn how to set time aside to read, fast, and pray. When God starts removing things and people from your life, don't be surprised. You will be learning how to live a more peaceful life. The bible says that the older you get, the wiser; it's time to grow up and put childish things away (1 Corinthians 13:11 NKJKV).

CHAPTER IV

EXAMINE YOURSELVES

Examine yourselves to see whether you are in the faith; test yourself. Do you not realize that Christ Jesus is in you – unless, of course, you fail the test? And I trust you will discover that we have not failed the test. Now we pray to God that you will not do any wrong – not so that people will see that we stood the test, but so that you may do what is right even though we may seem to have failed (2 Corinthians 13:5-7 NIV).

YOU HAVE NOT FAILED THE TEST

There is no such thing as failing a test with God. You might delay, but you have not failed. God doesn't leave us on a thin branch knowing it was going to break. We choose to stay because we think we know what's best for us. I'm here to tell you, "YOU DON'T."

We are so quick to say, "If I knew what I know now, I would have taken another route. "NOT TRUE." We still would've taken that same route because we want everything to be a quick fix. When a person's life turns upside down due to some of the wrong choices they have made, they tend to blame others. Some people will try and blame God, saying he brought evil upon them. You and only You did it to yourself and let's not leave out you tried to drag others along with you.

Until we learn how to stop blaming others for our downfalls wrong choices, causing us to be in that predicament; It will be less of a burden if we own up to our mistakes and fix them. If not, you will continue to live an unhappy, corrupt life.

For example, to keep the odor down in a sewer, they put lime in it to help control the smell, but after so long it begins to smell again. This is where some of us are with our life. We temporarily fix the probably but eventually go back to doing it again. Luckily, a few will stay on that straight and narrow path.

LEARNING TO GROW SPIRITUALLY

To be successful at something in life, you must study the material and put the work into it. When growing in your spiritual walk, this will require the same effort. You take what you learn and put it into your everyday living. Your relationship with God should be a full-time position.

We need air to breathe, food to live, and water to stay hydrated. We need God way more than all of these things because even though these items will keep you alive, you are still dead in the spirit.

Your walk with Christ will not be an easy journey because along the way, you will have to surrender on every level of your life. You will have to make choices about things you thought would be in your life forever.

COUNT IT ALL, JOY!

What do you mean? Glad you ask! When hired onto a job, specific training is required. After some time on the job, you are expected to execute all duties correctly. So, when you are reading God's word, you will learn how to operate in his will. You must learn how to obey and follow the instruction giving in the ten commandments (Exodus 20:2-17 NKJV) (Deuteronomy 5:6-21 NKJV).

Learn to know who God is, personally, mentally, and spiritually. The closer you draw to God, the closer he will draw to you (James 4:8 NKJV) (Jeremiah 29:12-14 NKJV). You will begin to build an intimate relationship with God. If you are doing these things, you will start to see a change in your life.

COUNT IT ALL JOY! (JAMES 1:2-8 NKJV)

ENCOURAGEMENT QUOTES

"If anyone or anything is costing your peace, get rid of it."
Shanika Shumpert

"You can never get back yesterday, but you can get it right
Today". Shanika Shumpert

"Anything that does not bring joy, peace, and happiness to
you, detach yourself from it and release it to God." Shanika
Shumpert

"Anything that's hindering you in your life, separate from it."
Shanika Shumpert

EXAMINE YOURSELF FIRST

Sometimes God uses other people to open our eyes to specific situations in our life. We are so quick to judge other people for their problems. If we're not walking in that person's shoes, we shouldn't speak about it because that person may be sick and silent at the same time. Here is a story with different problems but the same view.

Alana found out that her brother had been sleeping in a car, and he had a drinking problem. Alana is upset with her brother because, in her mind, she thinks he can suddenly stop drinking and do better for himself by not buying the alcohol and replacing it with water or a soda.

Alana doesn't understand that her brother is sick and doesn't know how to get help. One evening, Alana and her daughter Becky took a walk, and Alana's mom shared her feelings and opinions about her Brother with Becky. Becky knew she had to help her mom see that her sickness was no different than her brother's.

Becky begins to use her mom's sickness as an example. Becky states, to her mom, mom, you have diabetes, and you know that diabetes is a disease, and it will affect you eventually if you don't take care of yourself.
You still chose to eat unhealthy, knowing the consequence that follows later in life. If you want to live a long and healthy life, you must make a change. Alana's daughter made her realize that her situation was no different than her brother's. She helped her realize that they both had made a choice, healthier life-style or not.

We shouldn't be so quick to judge. Instead, we should examine ourselves before judging others. Alana was dealing with being a diabetic and wasn't taking care of herself, yet she was upset with her brother because of his alcoholism. She fail to realize that she was no better than her brother because she had a sickness and wasn't doing right by it either.

The next time you decide you want to judge a person on what they are doing or how they live, examine your own life first. I have learned that you can talk to a person until they are blue in the face. If they're not ready to make changes in their lives, There is nothing you can do or say to change their minds. Again, some people will receive the help, and some will not.

CHAPTER V
FORGIVENESS

Forgiveness is the less talked about topic in society today. No one wants to forgive but wants to be forgiven. It's crazy how forgiveness is set up in a person's mind.

Forgiveness is often talked about in the Bible. We must learn how to forgive one another. We want God to forgive us. If someone tells you that your fault is beyond anything they have ever seen and God won't forgive you, you rebuke them right there in the name of Jesus (Hebrew 10:17 NKLJV) because God forgives all sins (Psalm 103:12 NKJV). All sins are the same in our father's eyes. You must learn to forgive a person before you can live a peaceful and happy life. Because if you don't know how to forgive, then that person still controls a significant portion of your life.

If we want the Father to forgive us, we must forgive that person (Matt 6:15 NKJV). We all are saved by God's grace (Eph 2:8,9 NKJV). God wants us to love all people. We must love our enemies and pray for those who despitefully use us (Matt 5:44 NKJV). Learn how to replace hatred with love. (1 Cor 13:4-7 NKJV) Love is kind and patient. Love does not envy or boast; it is not arrogant or rude, and it goes on to say, love bears all things, believes all things, hopes all things, endures all things. Learn how to release your situation to God (Ps 55:22 NKJV). Learn how to forgive, so you can heal and move forward in life.

The inability to forgive can cause a person to live a miserable life. They never have anything good to say about the next person. They gossip about others etc. If I just described you, stop it. Stop letting people live rent-free in your mind.

Once you learn how to forgive and separate yourself from negativity and replace it with positivity then, you will begin to experience a life of peace. Sometimes, forgiveness is buried so deep inside of a person's mind that It takes a near-death experience just to open their eyes.

Always remember when you don't forgive, you hold yourself captive in the enemy camp because you allow hatred and unforgiveness to keep you there.

FORGIVENESS SCRIPTURE

If we confess our sins, he is faithful and just to forgive us for our sins and cleanse us from all unrighteousness (1 John 1:9 NKJV).

Bearing with one another, and forgiving one another, if anyone has a complaint against another; even as Christ forgave you, so you also must do (col 3:13 NKJV).

And whenever you stand praying, if you have anything against anyone, forgive him, that your Father in heaven may also forgive your trespasses (Mark 11:25 NKJV).

Therefore, if anyone is in Christ, he is a new creation; old things have passed away; behold, all things have become new (2 Cor 5:17 NKJV).

As far as the east from the west, so far has he removed our transgressions from us (Ps 103:12 NKJV).

Don't let anyone make you feel bad about your decision to follow God. Some people will make a mockery out of you, and that's ok. Ask God to give you the strength to be an overcomer.

Come now, and let us reason together, says the Lord: though your sins are like scarlet, they shall be as white as snow; though they are red like crimson, they shall be as wool (Isa 1:18 NKJV).

PRAYER OF FORGIVENESS

Lord, I come before you, asking for your forgiveness of my sins that I have committed knowingly and unknowingly. Lord, as I look back over my life, I have lived a life that was unpleasing to you. I have realized that I was travelling on a road that was leading me straight to hell. I know that you are a forgiving God. I ask that you come into my life and remove anything that is not of you out of me. I repent my sins and confess with my mouth unto you. I ask you to come into my life, clean me up, and teach me how to live a life pleasing to you. Please guide me on how to remove worldly things out of my way. Lord bless me with your wisdom, knowledge, and understand in the way you would want me to go. Strengthen me where I am weak, Lord. I want my heart to burn with the desire to live for you, in your Son Jesus name, Amen.

CHAPTER VI

SEPARATION

Separation is the action or state of moving or being moved apart. When dealing with problems that arise in our life, we begin to separate ourselves from people or situations that have shown their true identity.

When separating from someone or something, it can make you or break you. Sometimes, separation is a good way to gather your thought before making a big decision. For example, divorce happens because a problem had occurred that couldn't be solved.

Everybody wants to be right; no one wants to be wrong or admit being wrong. Most of our decisions are based off listening to others telling us what to do, which will cause you to make bad choices. Always remember that one bad mistake can last a lifetime, so when making a significant decision, let it be your choice. Do not let anyone influence you in your decision-making. Learn how to fast and pray in all that you do, learn to include God in all your decision-making.

Separation is sometimes best for a person; it gives them time to gather their thoughts. Sometimes we let our feelings get the best of us, and we make decision based off our emotions, and that's the worst mistake (1 Corinthians 15:33 NKJV). Do not be deceived: Bad company ruins good morals. When you are making a change in your life, you must separate yourself from, others.

(Romans 12:2 NKJV) says, "Do not be conformed to this world, but be transformed by the renewal of your mind." You can make changes in your life, but it will only last for a little while if your heart and mind haven't changed.

SEPARATION

When receiving food by the mouth, we break down the food by chewing it, so you can be able to swallow it. After consuming the food, it enters the stomach and the digestive system begin to break the food down by pulling the nutrient, vitamins, mineral, and sugar from it. Once this is done, the toxins that the body can't use (waste), is removed from the body through urine and bowel moment.

God's word is very similar to this process. We take it in by reading it. After reading His word, your analyze (break down) it. Then, you begin to apply His word to your everyday life. You begin to remove the things that are not Godly and replace them with things more pleasing to God. Once this takes place, you will start to see a change in your life. You will begin to feel a sense of peace over your life. You will begin to think and hear differently. Nothing will be able to hinder you from getting to the next level of your life.

After you have separated yourself from the things of the world, you will realize the ungodly life you were living. Separation is not something that happens overnight. When you are separating from the thing that is not of God, it will be a life challenge. Fasting and praying will take place when you begin to face trials in your life. Therefore, it's important to remove yourself from a negative environment and replace it with positive spiritual people. Praying will become a hobby in the season of separation. YOU GOT THIS!!!!

UNITY OF THE FAITH
EPHESIANS 4:13-16

Until we attain to the unity of the faith and the knowledge of the Son of God, to mature manhood, to the measure of the stature of the fullness of Christ, that we may no longer be children, tossed to and fro by the waves and carried about every wind of doctrine by human cunning, by craftiness in deceitful schemes. Rather, speaking the truth in love, we are to grow up in every way into him who is the head, into Christ, from whom the whole body, joined and held together by every joint with which it is equipped, when each part is working properly, makes the body grow so that it builds itself up in love.

ISOLATION

Isolation is when a person goes into hiding from their surroundings. It seems as if everything has turned upside down in that person's life, causing them to separate themselves from others. When It looks like there no hope, and no one understands what they are going through.

Isolation runs deep within a broken person who seems to have lost their way in life. Most people who go through this have experienced a deep hurt within themselves. When they are hurt deeply, they tend to separate themselves. They disappear from the visible world into the invisible world. Isolation is how people deal with the hurt. They remove themselves, but I'm here to tell you. Don't stop living because of life's issues. It's normal. You will experience hurt, heartache, and pain in this life on earth. The challenge is learning to heal from it. Stop running and hiding from it.

We must learn how to face our problems head-on, and the best way to equip ourselves is "KNOWING WHO GOD IS." When you discover who God is and what you mean to him, you will understand your power and authority through Jesus Christ, our Lord and Savior in your life. You will know how to live a life full of joy and peace.

CHAPTER VII
DELIVERANCE THROUGH CHRIST JESUS

God wants us to live a life free of sin and to be delivered from the stronghold of generational curses. God has given us the power and authority to cast out demons, break curses, and break strongholds (Matthew 10:1 NKJV). Deliverance is a process. It's' just like getting hired on a job. It's a process you must go through. Over the years, so many people have spoken by saying, it's no such thing as deliverance. I've come to tell you; there is a thing such as DELIVERANCE. I, firsthand, have experienced it. While getting deliverance from my sins, it almost cost me my life. I couldn't believe what had happened to me that night. I thought I was dying. Something came out of me. The next morning, I knew that God had delivered me by removing the evil spirits out of me. So, don't let anyone tell you there no such thing as deliverance.

When you begin the process of deliverance, you first must submit yourself to God (James 4:7-10 NKJV). Secondly, by asking God to come into your life, you must surrender to him (Galatians 2:20 NKJV). Thirdly, by asking God to come into your life and remove anything in you that is not of him. God will teach you His will and direct your path in the way He would want you to go (1 Peter 5:6-10 NKJV). Free yourself. Release your past and start a new beginning. Before you can go any further, you must get rid of your pride (Luke 9:23-24 NKJV) (Proverbs 3:5-6 NKJV).

When praying for deliverance, you must ask God to cleanse you from all your sins and remove anything in you that is not of him. David did. David had done everything under the sun, but God loved him because he was a man that went after God's heart.

David went to God in prayer. He poured out his heart to God, and God forgave him. David was forgiven for all his sins committed under ignorance and knowledge. If God did it for David, he would do it for you.

DAVID FORGIVENESS PRAYER TO THE LORD
(PSALMS 51: 1-6)

Have mercy upon me, O'God, according to your lovingkindness: according to the multitude of thy tender mercies blot out my transgressions. (David is confessing his sin to the Lord).

Wash me thoroughly from mine iniquity, and cleanse me from my sin. (David is asking God to forgive him for all his wrongdoing and cleanse him from the inside by forgiving him and giving him a new start with a clean and pure heart).

For I acknowledge my transgressions: and my sin is ever before me. (David is saying he knows he has done wrong and will never forget it, and he has learned from it).

Against thee, thee only, have I sinned, and done this evil in thy sight: that thou mightiest be justified when thou speakest and be clear when thou judgest. (David is telling God, not only have I sin against your will Lord, but I did it in your very sight).

Behold, I was sharpened in iniquity; and in sin did my mother conceive me. (David is saying that at birth, he was conceived through sin by his mother).

Behold, thou desires truth in the inward parts: and in the hidden part thou shalt make me, to know wisdom. (David is saying, God, I know that you take pleasure in honesty, but at birth, I was brought into this world in sin). (In so many words, David is trying to make up excuses, and he thought he could get away with it, by covering it up), but you still brought it to the light. I search for you in wisdom and truth. (David is pouring out his heart for God's grace and mercy, and forgiveness).

David was a man who loved God. If you haven't read the book of David, you must read it. Even though David was a mighty man of God, David was human. He was not perfect. None of us are walking perfections. We try to walk a good life with God, But it gets so overwhelming sometimes, causing us to go in another direction.

It causes us to commit sinful acts. And as long as we can get away with it, it appears ok. The very minute we get caught, we are sorrowful, and self-pity kicks in. Then, we are back in God's throne room. We're begging for forgiveness and pouring out our hearts to God. We're asking for his forgiveness, confessing our sins, and just because God is a forgiving God, he will forgive us.

Still, we must suffer for that sin. David got a married woman pregnant and tried to cover it up. But when it didn't work, everything fell apart. David realized that he had done wrong in God's very eyesight. He had forgotten that God is omniscient.

DAVID ASKING GOD TO CLEANSE HIM FROM HIS SIN (PSALM 51: 7-12)

Purge me with hyssop (the blood that transferred to the sinner by the death of Jesus Christ), and I shall be clean: wash me, and I shall be whiter than snow.

Make me hear joy and gladness; that the bones which thou hast broken may rejoice. (David is asking God to give him back his joy).

Hide thy face from my sins and blot out all mine iniquities (David is asking the Lord not to look at his sin anymore and to remove the guilt that he carried inside of him).

Create in me a clean heart, O'God; and renew in me a pure spirit within me. (make me whole in your very eyesight).

Cast me not away from thy salvation and uphold me with thy free spirit. (don't set me aside, Lord, let me show you I can be loyal to you again).

Restore unto me the joy of thy salvation and uphold me with thy free spirit. (Lord, give me back my joy and peace that I once had).

David was so caught up in covering up his sin that he forgot that God sees everything. If David had just gone to God and acknowledged his wrongdoing, it would have never grown so heavy on David's heart. We are just like David in today's society. When we are doing wrong, we try to cover it. We try to keep the secret until the secret gets too hard to bear.

Sometimes we try to keep that secret until we get upset. Only then do we want to let the cat out of the bag—just a temporary relief. We were already suffering in silence.

Now, we suffer even more. We suffer more because we come before public judgment. Don't put yourself in these situations. Just go to God. Confess, repent, and live an honest and righteous life. So, you don't carry a burden.

GIVING GOD PRAISE FOR HIS FORGIVENESS

(PSALM 51: 13-15)

Then I will teach transgressors thy ways; sinners shall be converted unto thee (restoring me Lord as your faithful servant again, so I can teach sinner how to turn back to you from their sins).

Deliver me from bloodguiltiness, O'God, thou God of my salvation: and my tongue shall sing aloud of the thy righteousness. (David is asking God to forgive him for the murder he committed, and he will forever give him praise).

O Lord, open thou, my lips; and my mouth shall show forth thy praise. (David is saying, as long as I have breath in my body, I will forever give you praise).

David not only committed adultery with Bathsheba by sleeping with her and getting her pregnant, but he also tried to cover it up. When it didn't work, he murdered her husband by sending him to the front-line in war to get killed. In David's prayer, he is asking God, to forgive him and make him pure in his eyesight again.

God has given all Christians the authority and the power to cast our demons. Just because you are Christians doesn't mean that you don't have an evil spirit in you. As Christian, we have to stay in God's word and obey his commandment. Are we going to fall short? Yes. Are we going to put things off? Yes. God is asking us to do right by him, and by that, he will do right by us. Here on earth, God wants us to live an honest and Godly life to the best of our ability.

GOD HAS GIVEN US SCRIPTURE THAT WILL HELP US WITH HEALING AND DELIVERANCE.

Heal me, O'Lord, and I shall be healed; Save me, and I shall be saved: For you are my praise (Jeremiah 17:14 NKJV).

The spirit of the Lord God is upon me because the Lord has anointed me to preach the good tidings to the poor; he has sent me to heal the brokenhearted, to proclaim liberty to the captives, and the opening of the prison to those who are bound (Isaiah 61:1 NKJV).

For the law of the spirit of life in Christ, Jesus has made us free from the law of sin and death (Romans 8:2 NKJV).

And you shall know the truth, and the truth shall make you free. Therefore, if the Son makes you free, you shall be free indeed (John 8:32,36 NKLJV).

Beloved, do not believe every spirit but evaluate the spirits, whether they are of God because many false prophets have gone out into the world (1 John 4:1 NKJV).

By this, you know the spirit of God: every spirit that confesses that Jesus Christ has come in the flesh is of God (1 John 4:2 NKJV). And every spirit that does not confess that Jesus is not from God is antichrist, which you heard is coming and is already in the world at this time (1 John 4:3 NKJV).

Little children are from God and have overcome them, for he who is in you is greater than he who is in the world (1 John 4:4 NKJV).

WHAT IS A DELIVERANCE PRAYER?

Deliverance prayer is a prayer asking God to remove evil spirits that dwell inside of you. You ask him to deliver you from strongholds, generational curses, diseases, mental illness, suicidal thoughts, drugs and alcohol addictions, fornication, adultery, murder, or any evils spirit that lives in you that you want God to cast it out. Strongholds are real, and they live inside of us.

Jesus casted out evil spirits throughout his walk here on earth. When delivering yourself, you must understand what you are doing because if you're not ready to live a full Christian life, that will give the demons access to re-enter back into your body, making them stronger.

The devil will use our weakest link to reel us back into the very same sinful act. Do your research on deliverance. You will hear it's no such thing as deliverance. YES, it is. If you apply yourself and trust God, I was delivered from a pervert sexual spirit. It came up out of me. It felt like something had separated from my body. It came out of my mouth, taking my breath away for a quick second.

It's hard to explain what I witnessed and felt at that moment, but I know it was real. Something came up out of me that night. When God delivered me, I begin to see a change in myself. I begin to love myself. I begin to live more.

We don't realize how much we have missed in life because we have a stronghold over our life. As you get stronger in Christ Jesus, your prayer life will become stronger, but right now, don't feel discouraged because God is not like man.

God accepts us as we are. We don't have to pretend. You go to him, whatever the issue that you're facing. God is a forgiving God who loves all his people.

DELIVERANCE PRAYER

Oh, heavenly Father, the Father of Abraham, Isaac, and Jacob. I come to you with a repentant heart, asking you to deliver me from my transgressions. Lord have mercy upon

me. My soul thirsts for you. Deliver me from the deceitful and

unjust man. Lord remember not my past. You search my heart

continually. Anything that you find in me that is unclean,

remove it. I cover my face with shame. Lord I plead for your

forgiveness. Have mercy upon me O'God, according to thy

lovingkindness: according to the multitude of thy tender

mercies. I blot out my transgression. Wash me thoroughly

from my iniquity. Cleanse me from my sin. Lord, I

acknowledge my wrongdoing, and I will never forget it. Lord, I

ask that you create in me a clean heart, renew my mind and

spirit within me. Cast me not away from your presence. Lord,
give me back my joy. You are the potter, and I am the clay.
Lord, make, shape, and mold me into the person that you
want me to be. I surrender myself to you. In your Son Jesus'
Name, I pray. Amen

CHAPTER III

PREPARATION

After the healing and deliverance process, and you come

out of isolation. You have prepared yourself to enter back into the world. Some people will fall off the road of recovery because the burden was too heavy to carry. What do you mean by that? Glad you ask! Because you cannot go back into the same toxic environment, you left. (remember, you are a new creature in Christ, your slate has been washed clean, sins are forgiven). If you are not strong enough, it will cause you to have a relapse. It will take no time for you to pick back up the habits and start right back off doing the same thing but worst. The devil will begin to play a mind game with you, making It seems as if your life was better before you surrender to God but don't fall for it, **DO NOT FALL FOR IT** it's the trick of the enemies trying to get in your mind.

It's so important during the healing process, that remove anything attached to you that is not of God.

Earlier I talked about isolation. Isolation is significant because you are making life changes. It will be such a disappointment to go back out into the world and start back where you left off. It will be such a shame to go through all of this just to fall back in the same situation. What you should do, get you a pen and paper after reading this and write it down (Ephesians 6:11-18 NKJV), or you can tear it out of this book and post it on your mirror and read it every morning and every night until you get it memories.

PUT ON THE WHOLE ARMOR OF GOD
CHAPTER 6:11-18

Put on the whole armor of God, that ye may be able to stand against the wiles of the devil.

For we wrestle not against flesh and blood, but against principalities, against powers, against the rulers of the darkness of this world, against spiritual wickedness in high places.

Wherefore take unto you the whole armor of God, that ye may be able to withstand in the evil day, and having done all, to stand.

Stand therefore, having your loins girt about with truth and having on the breastplate of righteousness.

And your feet shod with the preparation of the gospel of peace.

About all, taking the shield of faith, wherewith ye shall be able to quench all the fiery darts of the wicked.

And take the helmet of salvation, and the sword of the spirit, which is the word of God:

Praying always with all prayer and supplication in the spirit and watching thereunto with all perseverance and supplication for all saints.

REVELATION

We can't hide anything from God. He knows and sees everything we do. The Samaritan women at the well had an encounter with Jesus. He reveals everything she had ever done. The most beautiful part of all this is when Jesus tells her to go and sin no more (John 4:4-26 NKJV).

We don't need man's approval to be sin-free, but we do need God's approval and forgiveness. Revelation is a revealer; we need things to be revealed to understand our purpose here in this life.

When we are born into this world, we were born with a purpose from God. We don't understand it, but Satan does, and he knows if we grow into our purpose, it is not good for him. So, Satan seeks not to destroy us but the purpose that God has put over our life. So, Satan's job is to keep up from walking into it by introducing us to this world that is full of sin.

You cannot get what God has for you until you go through it. Betty Wright couldn't have written a better song: **"YOU GOT TO GO THROUGH SOMETHING IN ORDER TO BE SOMETHING."**

About the Author

Shanika Shumpert is a woman who wears many hats, mother of three, nurse, business owner, and founder of Broken But Yet Fixed Ministry. The Author is from Nettleton, Mississippi and her background is a wound care nurse in the medical field. She is a student of the Word and loves talking about God. What inspired Shanika in writing this book is the desire that burns inside of her to help draw people closer to God.

Made in the USA
Middletown, DE
24 June 2021